Membership of the Guide Movement breaks through all barriers between nationalities, colour, class and religious creed.

It also breaks through the barriers created by disability, for the fact that a girl cannot see, hear or walk need not stop her from becoming a Guide.

Even distance is no barrier. Girls in remote areas can join in Guide Meetings and Patrol Meetings by post.

To become a member of the Guide Movement is to join a great worldwide family; and friendships made will be friendships for life.

Acknowledgments:
The author and publishers wish to thank the Girl Guide Association for their help in the preparation of this book.
Acknowledgment is also made of the additional photographs and illustrative material: pages 5, 6, 23, 24-25 and front endpaper – John Moyes; pages 9, 10, 12, 13 – Girl Guide Association; page 43 and front endpaper – Alan Mears; page 39 – Chris Reed; page 11 – B H Robinson.

British Library Cataloguing in Publication Data

Scott, Nancy
   Girl guides.—Rev. ed.—(Hobbies)—
(Scouting; 4)
   1. Girl scouts—Great Britain
   I. Title   II. Series   III. Series
   369.46'3'0941   HS3353.G5

   ISBN 0-7214-0899-0

Revised edition

GIRL GUIDES

by NANCY SCOTT

photographs by JOAN RANDALL

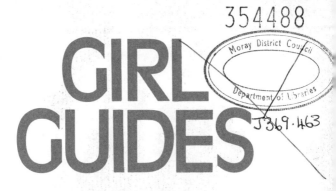

Ladybird Books Loughborough

The Promise Ceremony

What is a Guide?

Any girl over ten and under fifteen years of age can become a Guide. Some Guides may have spent several years as Brownie Guides and others may join a Company and be completely new to the idea of Guiding. It does not matter; every girl is welcome –

provided that she is willing to make the Promise that all Guides and Scouts make. It is the Promise which makes Guiding and Scouting a special kind of youth group.

The Promise Badge

4

Learning how to read a map

First, let us look at some of the things Guides do. They enjoy going to different places and finding out about things. They like to be out-of-doors as much as possible. They like to learn about people and history by visiting historic buildings and exploring ancient churches.

Guides have every opportunity to learn how to hike, climb, cycle and swim. They enjoy camping, where they learn how to live out-of-doors: pitching a tent, making a camp fire and cooking on it!

Pitching a tent

They learn how to follow a map, read a compass and how to recognise the tracks of wild creatures.

And to do all these things well, they must be fit, so Guides learn how to keep themselves healthy.

Tracking a fox

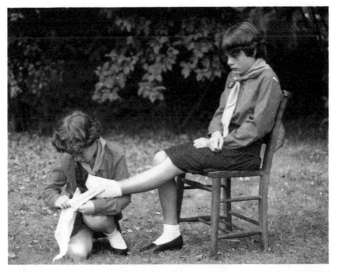

Practising first aid – treating a sprained ankle

They know how to help other people in times of danger or accident by learning many of the skills required in first aid and home nursing.

Guides are friendly people. They are able to make many new friends, not only in their own Patrol and Company, but by meeting Guides from other Companies, and corresponding with Guide pen-friends overseas. Their friendship goes beyond their own circle – to the elderly, handicapped, into children's homes and to lonely people.

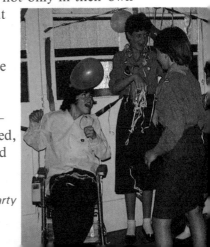

Girl Guides at a party

Guides enjoy creating things: drawing, painting, modelling, carving, writing, dancing, singing, acting, knitting, sewing. They give concerts, put on stage plays and help at bazaars and fêtes. There are many ways Guides use their creativity, for their own pleasure and to give pleasure and help to others.

Part of the Eight Point Programme: Exploring the Arts – music making

How Guiding began

Brownie Guides already know that the Scout and Guide Movement was started by Robert Baden-Powell who was an officer in the British Army. You can read more about this great man and the beginning of Scouts, Girl Guides and Brownie Guides in the Ladybird *Brownie Guides* book.

Scouting for boys began in 1907. Soon afterwards, girls formed their own groups, calling themselves Girl Scouts. But at that time it was not considered 'ladylike' for girls to do many of the vigorous and active things that boys enjoyed.

Robert Baden-Powell, who later became known throughout the Movement as B-P, did not wish to discourage girls from enjoying this new club he had invented for boys. If they also found it enjoyable, as they obviously did, judging by the enthusiasm with which groups were being formed all over the country, then they must be allowed to join in.

B-P decided that a separate Movement must be formed specially for girls, offering them a whole range of activities.

Lord Baden-Powell, founder of the Boy Scout and Girl Guide Movement

9

He hoped that the girls joining the Movement would combine the more traditional home-making skills, such as cooking and sewing, with the exciting outdoor pursuits enjoyed by Scouts.

B-P retired from the army in 1910 to devote all his energy to the Boy Scouts. As his time was fully taken up with the fast-growing Scout Movement, he asked his sister Agnes to organise the new Movement for girls, and to undertake the work of adapting his book *Scouting for Boys* to make it suitable for them.

Agnes Baden-Powell was a talented woman and like all the members of her family she used and developed her talents to the full. She was a good musician and artist, and skilled in many of the homecrafts and handicrafts of her day.

She was particularly interested in natural history, and always kept a variety of pets. For instance, she

kept bees in a glass hive in her London house. They made their way out to the park and back via a pipe laid through a hole in the wall! The honey they made won prizes at several exhibitions. She also kept a colony of *live* butterflies,

Agnes Baden-Powell, the first President of the Girl Guide Movement

Some of the first Girl Guides

rather than the dead pinned specimens collected by many people at that time. In the hall of her house several small birds flew freely.

In trying to organise this new Movement for girls, Agnes Baden-Powell had to fight many battles against the prejudices of the day. Although the girls themselves were keen, many parents and other adults in authority were convinced that Guiding would turn girls into tomboys.

But such was the strength of Agnes Baden-Powell's personality and enthusiasm that she soon gained many supporters. She went on to become the first President of the new Movement.

Olave, Lady Baden-Powell, who married B-P in 1912, helped her husband with the new Girl Guides. She was made Chief Guide in 1918 and World Chief Guide in 1930

B-P called this new Movement the *Girl Guides* and in May 1910 the first official Headquarters Committee for the Girl Guide Movement was formed. B-P took the word *Guide* from two sources.

The first came from a famous corps of guides in India: men known for their general hardiness, their resourcefulness in dealing with difficult situations, their keenness and courage. They were a force trained to take up any duties required of them, and could turn their hands to anything.

The second source for the name came from the mountaineering guides, working in Switzerland and other mountainous regions: men who could guide people, with bravery and skill, over the most difficult and dangerous territory.

So, said B-P, the word *Guide* had come to mean one who possesses all these good qualities, including industry, common sense, and self-reliance. It is these qualities that Guides, down the years, have tried to gain through an interesting programme of training and service to others.

Worldwide Guiding

The Guide and Scout Movement began in Great Britain, but its reputation and popularity soon spread to other countries.

The United States was one of the first countries to take it up. Mrs Juliette Low, a friend of the Baden-Powells, was one of the early pioneers of Guiding and Scouting. She had already started several Companies in Great Britain before returning to her native town, Savannah in the state of Georgia, USA, in 1912. There she gathered together a group of girls and told them about the new Guides in Britain. Soon these girls wanted a troop of their own. So Juliette Low made what has since become known as her 'famous phone call', to a friend saying: 'Come right over. I have got something for the girls of Savannah, and all America, and all the world, and we are going to begin tonight.'

How right she was! From thousands in Britain, the Movement grew to several million throughout the world, and in 1928 the big Guide-family officially took the name *The World Association of Girl Guides and Girl Scouts*. Some countries, for example, the United States, still prefer to keep the earlier name of Girl Scouts.

Mrs Juliette Low

13

Guides from different countries gather at an International Camp – a Belgian Guide (left) tries lace making

Although the uniform varies throughout the world, all members of the World Association have a motto, many sharing the same one. All Guides greet each other with the same sign or salute – three raised fingers – which reminds them of their

A Japanese Guide joins in a leatherwork session

Promise. They all wear the trefoil in the Promise Badge and use the left handshake of friendship. Any Guide who has attended a World Camp or Conference will tell you how valuable these shared signs and a warm smile can be in bridging the gap between races and creating a friendly family feeling.

Norwegian Guides help to roll up a brass-rubbing

15

The Promise

The strength of Guiding lies in the Promise which all Guides and Girl Scouts make, and do their best to keep. The Promise gives them a purpose in life, a way to follow.

Every Guide who makes this Promise is *trusted* to do her best to keep it. The words 'do her best' are very important.

A Guide promises *to do her best* in all she says, does, and thinks – not just when she is in uniform or at a Guide Meeting, but every day, everywhere.

Every girl who becomes a Guide accepts the Promise as a challenge, but she knows that she is not alone in trying to do her best to live up to the high standard set, for she has a great worldwide family of friends to support and encourage her.

The actual words of the Promise vary a little between one country and another, but their meaning and spirit are the same.

Guides at a church service

All put service to God first, then service to a Guide's own country, and to other people. Finally, the Guide promises to try to keep the Guide Law.

The Law

The Guide Law makes ten positive statements. It does not say what a Guide may be, or can be, or should be – it states what she *is*. This is the foundation of Guiding.

1 A Guide is loyal and can be trusted.

2 A Guide is helpful.

3 A Guide is polite and considerate.

4 A Guide is friendly and a sister to all Guides.

5 A Guide is kind to animals and respects all living things.

6 A Guide is obedient.

7 A Guide has courage and is cheerful in all difficulties.

8 A Guide makes good use of her time.

9 A Guide takes care of her own possessions and those of other people.

10 A Guide is self-controlled in all she thinks, says, and does.

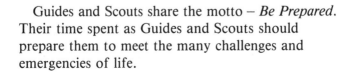

Guides and Scouts share the motto – *Be Prepared*. Their time spent as Guides and Scouts should prepare them to meet the many challenges and emergencies of life.

A new member is welcomed into her Patrol

The Patrol

All Guide Companies are made up of a number of Patrols. A Patrol is a small group of four to eight Guides, with a Patrol Leader chosen by the members of that Patrol, and a Patrol Second who is chosen by the Leader.

A new Guide is welcomed into a Patrol and most of her Guiding activities will be done with this same group of people. A successful Patrol is one where every member 'does her best' and shares fully in its work and play.

Patrols are usually called after birds, flowers, or trees. In long-established Companies, such names are rarely changed because they have become traditional and have many 'Old Guides' linked to them.

In many cases, trophies won by the Patrol in the past will be inscribed with their name, colours and emblems. But a new Company sometimes likes to be up to date and invent new names for its Patrols, and it is free to do so, provided the names chosen are inspiring, attractive and have some lasting value. Since a Guide wears the emblem of her Patrol on her uniform, the name of a new Patrol must be one which can be well illustrated on the badge.

Robin Patrol emblem

The Patrol Leader encourages and helps members in the group and makes sure that Guiding in *her* Patrol is challenging and fun for everyone. She also represents the Patrol at the Patrol Leaders' Council.

The Patrol Second's job is to assist the Leader in every way she can, and also to take charge should the Leader be away at any time.

A good Leader will arrange for other members of the Patrol to do certain jobs, rather than try to do everything herself. For instance, if the Patrol decides to keep a log book of their activities, then someone will be appointed Secretary.

The Patrol Secretary will then be responsible for writing up the log book, or she may ask other members of the Patrol to write items to go in it. She will also write any Patrol letters that may be necessary.

A Patrol member who is good at drawing and painting will become the Patrol artist, illustrating the log book, decorating the equipment and notepaper, etc. Another member may be appointed Treasurer. Her job will be to collect and record the money that the Patrol members contribute to Patrol funds.

Two new Guides, one coming to Guiding for the first time, the other an ex-Brownie Guide, are shown a Patrol log book

A Patrol artist records the purchase of new Patrol colours

Patrol meetings

A Patrol not only meets at the weekly Company meetings, but tries to hold its own regular meetings at other times. These are the greatest fun of all, because the members themselves choose what they want to do, how to do it, and where they want to go. Any activities which a Patrol plans to do on its own will depend on where the members can meet, the weather and time of year.

Indoor and winter meetings are ideal times to become proficient at handicraft skills, such as toy-making. This could be combined with a special good turn, by giving the toys made to a local children's home or hospital.

Learning how to wire up plugs

Lighting a fire in winter

Even in winter it is possible to hold Patrol meetings outdoors by planning a hike to a place of particular interest such as an old church or disused railway cutting (an interesting place for nature study). This would provide opportunities for sketching, photography, map and compass reading. A great deal of ground can be covered on a winter hike, because it is necessary to keep on the move in cold weather! And landmarks are more obvious when the trees and bushes are bare.

An outdoor meeting in a garden or park provides an ideal opportunity to practise, for example, running, jumping, ball throwing or rope throwing, in preparation for an athletics test.

A Patrol, always keeping in mind the importance of giving service to others, might plan to tidy the garden of an elderly, sick or infirm person. Or they

Guides and Brownie Guides put on a Christmas show

may decide to put on a short concert to entertain a
senior citizens' club or retirement home.

Fund raising

A Patrol can decide to train for some particular event as a single unit. Whatever the project, it will require careful thought and planning and the whole Patrol must work together, making use of each Guide's own special ability, from the newest member to the experienced Patrol Leader.

All Guides pay a regular subscription to Company funds. Part of this money is used to finance the Company and pay for equipment, part is sent to the Regional Headquarters for supporting and promoting Guiding in their County, and part is sent to Guide Commonwealth Headquarters to meet organisational expenses.

Regular subscriptions to Company funds and to Patrol funds are often not enough to meet the needs of a lively Company, and so different ways to raise more money have to be found.

In olden times, when knights went out on their missions, they were ordered to be thrifty and to earn money when they needed it, instead of being a burden to others. They also earned money to give away to those in need. B-P believed that Guides and Scouts should follow their example.

Earning money can be fun especially when everyone works together. If money is needed quickly, then a Jumble Sale is one of the easiest events to organise. A Bring-and-Buy Sale can be combined with a coffee evening or morning, giving some Guides the opportunity to gain hostess skills.

Making puppets to sell at a summer fête

A Christmas Bazaar or a Spring Fair can be great fun to work for, giving a Guide lots of opportunities to use different skills, such as doll-dressing, toy-making, sweet and jam-making, baking cakes, and growing boxes of seedlings, bowls of bulbs and plants of all kinds. A wide-awake Company, discussing and pooling their ideas, can think up many novelty stalls to add to the attraction of the Fair.

Making sugar hedgehogs to raise money for Patrol funds

Charity work

Collecting used items to help a chosen charity is something Guides are very good at. Clean milk bottle tops, or used postage stamps which have been carefully cut off envelopes, leaving the perforated edges of the stamps themselves intact,

are always welcomed by certain charity organisations. Such collections are often much easier to organise in a Patrol than in the Company as a whole – every member of the Patrol pledging herself to take part, and handing her contribution each week to a Patrol Collector.

On the toy stall.

Not only do Guides earn money for their own needs but, remembering the knights of old, they earn and save money to help people less fortunate than themselves, in their own country, and in other countries where help is needed.

Sorting and bundling newspapers in aid of District funds

A Company may decide to help a local cause or, through the Girl Guide Friendship Fund, they may help in a much larger project.

One such project was called 'Saving Sight'. It was discovered that the cause of so much distressing blindness in Indian babies was due to a Vitamin A deficiency. Vitamin A is found in green vegetables, but green vegetables are scarce in parts of India, and so is money. Yet just one cupful of green vegetable taken every day would both prevent and cure this blindness. An appeal was launched through the Guide and Brownie Guide magazines, asking for £5,000.

Within a few months not only had the £5,000 been raised by Guides and Brownie Guides, but they had doubled that figure to £10,000! The money was raised in often quite remarkable and even amusing ways. It must have been great fun too!

Can you imagine the number of shells that had first to be collected, then washed and sorted, to make 255 perfect shell mice? Can you walk on stilts? One Patrol mastered this particularly difficult balancing act, and held a sponsored Stilt-walk in an empty car park.

Another Company held a sponsored Knit-in. This involved collecting wool, getting willing sponsors, and then practising knitting until they became really proficient. At the Knit-in itself they knitted as many equal-sized squares as they could within a given time. Afterwards the squares were sewn together to make warm blankets for elderly people.

Everything a Guide does comes back to the importance of the Patrol in the first place, for nearly all schemes begin from discussions and ideas raised at Patrol Meetings.

Badges

A Guide need never be at a loss for something interesting and worthwhile to do. She has only to explore the pages of the *Guide Handbook* to find lots of ideas and suggestions for challenging and interesting things she can tackle, all aimed at developing her skills and knowledge.

Working for the Child Nurse Badge

A Guide is tested for the Photographer Badge

All the badges worn on a Guide's uniform have a special meaning or purpose. Some are the insignia of a Guide's membership; for example, the Promise Badge (see page 4), the title tape showing the name of her Company, the County Badge and her Patrol Emblem. Other badges show her progress in Guiding.

Interest badges cover a wide variety of interests and encourage a Guide to learn new hobbies and skills – dancing, singing, photography, gardening, writing, playing an instrument, drawing and painting, watching birds, camp-craft, braille for the blind, manual alphabet for the deaf, cooking, knitting and signalling are just a few of the subjects on offer.

In addition to these, there are *Service* badges which call for a very high and consistent standard of service to others, including first aid and home nursing, where a Guide must learn to act promptly and sensibly in an emergency.

Camp

CAMP – a magic word for so many Guides! Here is the chance to spend a whole thrilling week or more with friends, and experience the fun of life under canvas.

Testing the bedding rack

A Guide can put into full practice so many things that she may have only experimented with in the garden, park or playground. Pitching a tent that you are actually going to sleep in is far more exciting than merely putting one up to discover how to do it. There is, too, a definite art to rolling up camp bedding and stacking it neatly clear of the ground by day, on a gadget you have made yourself.

You then quickly discover if your woodcraft skill in selecting wood and lashing the parts together is up to standard – or not! Gadgets which look so sturdy, strong and neat when you first erect them, often have a nasty habit of collapsing under the weight of a roll of bedding! But it's all part of the fun, and everyone learns quickly from their mistakes!

Making a rope bridge

Building a shelter

A camp kitchen is very different from the kitchen at home and offers plenty of opportunities for amusing 'disasters'. Even a stew, slightly burnt on the bottom of the dixie, and potatoes that you have peeled yourself, nicking your fingers at the same time, can taste quite different and surprisingly good when cooked over a camp-kitchen fire or stove.

Patrol cooking at camp

Appetites become so enormous when living out-of-doors that there is no place for finickiness over food.

Guides enjoy a well-earned break

At camp, a Guide can discover the beauty and wonder of the stars, perhaps for the first time in her life. She can take part in *Wide Games*. These are games covering a wide area of land, perhaps involving tracking skills. She may put into practice her knowledge of map reading, following compass directions, perhaps to find a hidden treasure, or using strategy to capture another Patrol's stronghold. She might have a chance to visit a local farm to learn something about the busy life of the farmer, his wife and helpers.

Planning an expedition

Around the campfire

The highlight of camp life is always the campfire entertainments and sing song in the evenings. To sit round a big blazing fire, in the cool of the evening, perhaps with the glorious smell of potatoes baking in their jackets among the embers, is so enjoyable that no words can describe it.

Guides have a special hymn they sing at the close of all Guiding events, called *Taps*. This word came from the American army, where the tapping on a drum was used as a signal, telling the men that it was time to go to bed. Later the signal became a bugle call, but the original name was kept.

To hear Taps sung around the dying embers of a campfire last thing at night is an experience few Guides, or visitors, will ever forget.

The hymn has a special significance and meaning in such a setting. It ends with the words, 'God is nigh,' and this is a belief that all Guides share. 'I promise to do my duty to God' is the first part of the Promise that a Guide makes, and in saying this she is putting God in His rightful place – *first* in her life.

Many Guide Companies attend a religious service once a month with their local Youth Organisations, and a Guide finds this helpful in getting to know more about God and discovering how best she can serve Him.

Day is done,
Gone the sun,
From the sea,
From the hills,
From the sky.
All is well,
Safely rest,
God is nigh.

The Brownie Guide Promise

Service to others

One way in which a Guide serves God is by developing the skills He has given her, and using them to help others.

The idea of service begins in Brownie Guides when a new member, at her Brownie Promise Ceremony, recites the Law. This is, 'A Brownie Guide thinks of others before herself and does a

Good Turn every day.' When she becomes a Guide she is expected to do *at least* one good turn every day, but whereas a Brownie Guide may be encouraged to record and talk about her good turns with the Guider in charge, so developing a good habit, a Guide does not talk about them to others.

A Guide just does them as quietly and efficiently as she can, without thought of any reward. Maybe the good turn will be a simple one, like noticing if someone is following her through a door and holding it open for them instead of letting it slam back in their face; or it may be a more spectacular good turn, such as pulling a drowning child out of a river. Both are good turns, the first depending on the development of thoughtfulness and consideration for others, the second on the development of quick thinking and physical skill.

A Guide helps Brownie Guides to make nature collages

Ranger Guides

A Guide may stay in the Guide Company until her fifteenth birthday, but between the ages of fourteen and fifteen she may go on into a Ranger Guide Unit if there is one in her District. There she will find that new activities and fresh adventures await her, but in a more adult setting. At her Investiture, a Ranger Guide affirms that her special responsibility as a Ranger is to be of service in the community. She is now 'looking wider', as the Founder of the Movement, Robert Baden-Powell, urged all Guides and Scouts to do.

Flower arranging

In the Ranger Guide Unit she will have opportunities to develop the skills she has learnt in the Guide Company to a higher level: skills in first

Rock climbing during Rangers' Activity Week

aid and home nursing, housecraft and child care and creative crafts. She will have opportunities for greater adventures, perhaps exploring the countryside on horseback, discovering the thrills of canoeing, or the exhilaration of mountain and rock climbing. She will have the companionship of camping and other social events with Venture Scouts, visiting Rangers in other countries, learning to service and fly a plane, sail a boat, service a car, or ski proficiently.

But holding together all the interesting exciting adventures, and worthwhile things a Guide or Ranger Guide does, is the Promise – the foundation of all Guiding and Scouting.

Index